Lost City Highway

by

Jake St. John

A Jabber Publication

A Jabber Publication
P.O. Box 299
Columbia, Ca 95310

Paperback # 7

Ed. 1

ISBN: 9781794133167

Cover by Andy Heck Boyd

To my children

American Stranger

Hands buried
in the pockets
of his worn
tattered denims
his duffel
packed only
with journals
and an old
beaten copy
of a *Road* book

Thoughts drift
to the town
miles down
the ancient road
the one that
flashed by
his passenger window
hours ago
preceding
the conclusion
of a transient
gesture

The image fades
and the future emerges
from the desert night

Unknown and glorious
The Hitchhiker continues
his rebellious tour
into America

Boots scuffle over sand
watched by desert life

2

dreams caught
in the cool air

A dark silhouette
pierces the painted sky
dawn looms bringing dead deeds
swirling into his head

the past is a creature
in no need of sleep

A rusted red pickup
welcomes the Hitchhiker
at sunup
a silent flick of a thumb
The Hitchhiker
nests down
in the truck bed
the window slides open
the gray driver
takes in his guest

How far you going?
Far as I can
How'd you get out here son?
Anyway I could
(Nod)

The truck takes motion
a dusty trail wind
fades into history
The Hitchhiker
eases his eye

Life Views from Bourbon Street, Reflecting

Stealing the night
He wears it like a mask

Slow streets slump
   And wait to be born

Do you know how to feel
   And what is at stake?

I see sin through thin disguise
   And smile

The sidewalks are our spies
    Screaming for sweet surrender

Brick film screens
   Showing a picture I've seen before

    Poetry
    Poverty
    Purity

Look
  she's nude
  in the window!

I think we're still wet from birth

Even a cricket casts a large shadow
    In the right light

Are the gates open for our escape?
We're unknown in India

Sex chased a couple into the alley, laughing

Can I make it to California?

I tease myself with a clear thought
                    But she's quick to leave
              Loners
              Lovers
              And the Lost
Whose tears are these?

Poem for New London

I walk to town
to figure out my head
and see the beauty
in this wailing city
of poets artists
lunatics and saints

Light rain falls
in slight patterns
and I cannot hide
the stars have gone away
like the eyes of strangers
when I look at them

Past the drug corporation
now in its death throes
the luminous burn of street lamps
neon shining through windows
white coats at work
designing fashionable pills
for the dysfunction of the day

I hear the whistle
of the rattling passenger cars
rumbling through overpass overhead
taking my dreams down the tracks
and around the bend into tomorrow

I can see the buildings
and hear the rush of cars
just past Shaw's Cove
and if you listen
really listen
you can hear the music of the city

Ruminations Out Loud

Be your own voice
and open your eyes
I said
stumbling from a higher plane
cutting holes in life
with a Diamond

and this city
with early morning blessings
golden splintered light
rising out of the sea
is absolute
in its Emptiness

who will be buried with a smile

there is equality
in our essence
a relation to the end
the difference is thought

have you heard the sound
of a snowflake falling
on a mountain peak

The Death of My Grandfather, Reading Philip Whalen

I had no guests
last night

the sun moved
and I sat still
or I should say
I sat still
moving around the sun

I haven't made my bed
in weeks

Golden Eternity
I'm no good with change

all these flowers
and no poems

Lost World

We find
ourselves
alone
reaching
for a dream
on the brink
of reality

hopelessly lost
in a cruel wilderness

why is your smile
so tame?

our lucid expectations
of the dawn
burn like a candle

this pale tragedy
falls like stardust
into the bright night

where is the western promise of love?

Satori

Woke up
and got drunk
found my way to the streets
and tripped along the tracks
passed a café
I read poetry at
when I was you

and nothing was empty

and a car in the street

and horns

and disruption

$2 in my pocket
enough for black coffee
and the paper
it's full of news
I can get for free
with my eyes open
and my ears to the ground

and somewhere

on a television

the State of the Union
is being read

and I
    did
        not
            listen

Life is Dust

How many petals
make a flower?
now it's autumn
and they're dead
but they're flowers
nonetheless

Subterranean Skyline

It's 8:40pm
and I'm on a rooftop
in New London
I can't describe the stars
and how they blink like eyes
overhead
but they're still right there

and I can't help staring

and everyone's talking

and I hear it all

every word

every thought

and I know I'm young
and callow
too arrogant to notice
that I've gotten older
with the turn of a page
and Dead River Time
who trickled thinly
through the years
has risen above the levee

Dead Have Eyes

I see
more crows
every day

Not flapping
or squawking
or strutting
or walking

but sitting
and staring

as if they know me

Today,
Reading Ted Berrigan

I am envious
of elephants

I have a difficult time
remembering the morning

Don't mention
past lives

I do remember
a time of mourning

I read what you wrote
and I'm scared
that I am a person
of the future

I haven't heard
a good joke
in a while

Lost City Blues

Head down
and walking
on damp sidewalks
that seem to clatter
all the way
to the inside shadows
and around corners

streets from nowhere
with family names
that don't exist anymore
sneak up on me

I'm slightly
nerved and aware
chomping down
on grains of sand
my jaw swollen
and tense
from not having
any dreams
or at least the ones
that stick around

Cobble stones
peak up
through potholes
paintings crawl
across brick walls
giving people
the creeps
even the freaks
are ignored these days

Dreams of Esperanza

It's late
and I'm walking
the Mexico City streets
with ol' Jack
he's on morphine
and the storm
has him soaked
but I am too
but only because
the sky
rains down
truth
and my cheeks
are deserts

but inside
the floods
recede
and a tidal wave
crashes
on my heart

Dream Angels

Went to bed
had poems
scratched
on my eyes

When I rise
vanish
woke up in a coffin
spitting nightmares
off my tongue

My head
is less than perfect
nothing is still
or moving

Teeth turn to dust
weigh the possibilities
I can't grasp
The magnificent sorrow
of space

The unending timetable
of existence
talking to the dead
in silence

New London, Exquisite

Dim alleys
and side streets
alive
with random melody

The train rattles
and slows
carrying drifters
to our coast

Feet step lightly
on painted walkways
adrift
in great delusion

Couples silent
silhouetted
by cigarette smoke
embrace on the pier

Satyrs roam
with arrogant intention
seeking
soiled pleasure

The artist has grace
an honorable philosophy
misunderstood
by conventional perception

The Electric Philosopher

The Strange Man enters the night
with the moon his only wife

Smoldering dreams play cruel games
in the soft streets

Regretting untimed thought
and wasted days
silent words
and unused wisdom

The Strange Man sits alone in a cave
high in the hills
stuck in thought

Winter ways
suffocate hope

Insane nights shatter
in neon prisms

Following the Green Sheppard
in soulless marches
the dead on display

Broken pyramids and false legends
dead in alleys

Attempting to avoid glass values
with spider webs of poison doubt

The Strange Man sits

Morning Sun

Shadows ease
through this
paradise

sitting
with a dream
in my eye
staring east

waiting
for Heaven's eye
to burn
the horizon

knowing that
dawn's beauty
falls
when balanced
against you

Eye of the Storm

Winter brings snow
to the long grass meadow
and maze of bone

Dark as the sea
we are grey clouds
flying in a sky of stars

Poem for Honesty

Waiting
for the open winds
to blow away
tomorrow
from my memory

neon scars
in shadows
won't wipe clean

shooting stars
leave dust
in my eyes

"This town
fell off
a charm bracelet"

and landed
in a puddle
of red wine

it's a sad world
when tongues
are perfect

Cosmic Baseball

2 down
in the bottom
of the night
the moon floats
like a great big
knuckleball
I put the poem
in play
and the stars erupt
the sun begins
to warm up
in the pen

Folded Paper
for Tom Weigel & Bambino Spinelli

Two Italians exchanging money
"This ain't no drug deal"

This is different
There's more to it than that

The lamb is not over cooked
But we might be

Turn us over
And slap our backs

Maybe we'll get lucky

Harmonica Poem

I carry a harmonica
in my back pocket
to pass the time

I can't play much
but I can make noise
like everybody else

what's better
it lets you know
that I'm here

because
if I don't tell you
who will?

Awakening

The words
came from
her mouth
with every
intention
of pain
and to her
it was only
a passing
comment
but to me
it was
everything
I needed
to hear

To Love

Surrender
all capacity
of knowing

a contrast
in vision

until
not 1
but 2

or more

revolving
on a dependence

to the whole

Reflection on Self
While Thinking of California

Back from tomorrow
and my legs
ache with weariness

distracted
by the loneliness
of movement

leaves scatter
downwards in wind
scratching at the road

standing in the garden
under yellow moon
above glass sound

I am a molecule
in the immense body
of being

understanding distance
in relation to space
all things plausible

attainable with proper design

The Anarchy of Stars

We will never find home
in the same manner
we once knew

somehow we try
in ways we do not realize
occurring on the edges of cobwebs
memories of sleep

the far distant beginning
happens daily
the farther we walk
to the infinite
no closer do we appear

About You

I sit
at a table
alone
with my beer

listening to
a conversation
about tuning
a mandolin

and thinking
how I would
love to tune
these words

and make
them sing
the way I do
when thinking

about you

Saturday Night

Walking by the bar
flannel haired hipsters
standing cool
in blue clouds
of smoke
conversations
drowned out
by the latest
collaboration
of musicians
discussing
future gigs
and politics
in the cold

Yesterday

Seems far removed
from today
but the leaves
are now falling
from the recently
potted plants
the photographs
have worn
at the corners
and faded slightly
over the young faces
who have now seen
many years since
the meticulous crawl
of westward expansion

Old Young

All the dreams
you never had
are tangled
in your eyes
and briefly escape
hidden under
the words
that slip
from your tongue

Spirit

You belong
out there
among the
wildflowers
that grow along
pine shadowed
streams
and crawl
slowly down
sunlit slopes
and fall
silently
into a
granite sea
but here
you are
with me
and for that
I apologize

On My Way to Work

I stopped to admire
a large turtle
on the side
of the hayfield road
this morning

he was resting
comfortably
under the overcast sky
we both knew
it would rain soon

as I moved along
up the hill
he sat motionless
going nowhere
at his own pace

From My Desk by the Window

The glowing orb in the silken sky
brightens the upturned leaves
that flutter upwards
by the empty playground

where school children will
laugh and scream with green knees
and run towards the wind
until all noise is absent

only they can feel the lightness
of air within innocent gallops
as small feet touch down
upon dandelion grass

youthful hours are not understood
until the body is lacking time
and the mind grasps the essence
of being completely and vividly alive

Summer's End

From my porch
the trees break
in part enough
to bring into view
one drunken boat
wobbling
among the waves

Vastness of Terrain

Seeing how
the land lays
the connection
we have
is roots

in moments
like these
time seems
to slow

and low
touching winds
kick leaves
over neighboring
hills
to the sea

and a storm
waves them
goodbye

Change of Address

After we
disappear

we come back
again

only briefly
an eternal second

emerging in
the vacant corner

of a familiar eye
just to inspire

a thought
before leaving

Old Friend Night

Streets damp with moonlight
                    are silenced
I'm silenced

I remember when my boots
                    still had soul
and I could think
but not real thoughts

now they squeak
                    in the rain
all time
                    is eternity
and the moon
                    is smiling holy
tonight

Song

I'll go out alone
                with you
tonight

I disappear for only
                a second
to clear my head

timing is all we have
                in the end

the nocturnal rhythm of tides
                beats a complex cadence
                on the heart
the minding numbing chaos
                of waking
weighs heavily on my eyes

my shoulders slouch
and carry the burden of rising torches

the even tempo of clouds

the overrun of stars
                is lightened
in your steps

and the moment of hope
                is outlined
in a primitive moon.

East at Night

The moon is upon the city
        brilliant
is the black silence
        of stars
neon glare
from tavern windows
        reflects
in the street of mirrors

hissing and wheezing
        echo
in paved valleys

cars dash through life
unexpected beauty
        blurred
and fading in the rearview

cigarettes fall
        from passing windows
dancing in the dark
        exploding on contact
like fireworks
        celebrating
        some unknown victory

visitors keep to street lights
        selling their soul
        for warm beer
and mini skirts
        while an electric melody
tumbles out a pub door
into the escapade of night

42

Driving in the Rain

The road
ahead
paved
in red
brake lights
wet sidewalks
margin
the street
yellow lights
of buildings
blurred
through raindrops
like fireflies
caught out
in a storm
the traffic light
hanging above
like an old
gatekeeper
turned green
I lurched
forward
into the white
light
of the moon

Of The West

I

I close my eyes
awaken to a fast paced nightmare
alarm clocks
suits in cars
droning
presidents dead and buried
leave me lonely

east coast visions
high speed breathing
no time for flowers

city anxious
off beat uneasy
chasing Buddha

search for green grass
on asphalt fields
transient escape

hop the train to dharma
ride the rails to reason's edge
acknowledge the stars

II

Strip mine your past America
burn your morals at the industrial altar
desperate and mad, naked to the soul

Iraq lurches in my stomach

media skin
media eyes
controlled visions

"let us do the thinking for you"

the revolution will be low frequency
can you hear the drums?

open corridors
zigzagging death
ghosts of culture

discount enlightenment
sell happiness with a shrug

III

Blacktop freedom
curving through dreams
awake on the far side of the river
conjure desires with the dawn

tranquil smiles at the village gates

> *"who are the wide eyed strangers
>   and what gifts do they bring?"*

IV

A cerulean sheet, draped over the parched floor
wandering in hopeless joy, rationally disoriented
bound to the Earth, conceived in her womb
born into Eden

has the broken road of awareness
fallen from grace?

adrift in the erratic spirit of wilderness
declaring allegiance to the desert
the artifact of culture
buried in the ruins
bleeding in the face of God

a bourbon and marijuana mask

facing the hostile lavender horizon

swirling and pulsing
rolling through the twilight

electric flares from Heaven
blackened dunes outlined
bright
violent amethyst sky
seared in memory

V

Write your soul across the arid page
bare and receptive, limitless in your freedom

consciously discover the veiled individual
transcend veracity, breathe

VI

Tracking the beach, pursuing lust with a smile
spirits with relaxed wings
receive visitors
to their shores
of surreal currents

congested highways
high speeds
rubber on maddening road
the apex of history, the last valid revolution

the perception of beauty upon rough diamonds
the strange interpretation of aesthetics

smoothly transfixed by delusion
and the artful hold of pacific seas
the eternal imprint of the western dream
engraved on the core of human essence

the radiance at the spectrum's end
mirrored in converse eyes
true enlightenment

VII

I hunger for democracy
I hunger for hysterical prophets
I hunger for ambivalent minds to grow legs and stand

I hunger for unknowing midnight
getting drunk in alleys with poets
leaving half full glasses of beer
for the homeless

I hunger for the child left behind for his own benefit
I hunger for my children
never having to ask

What is a forest?

I hunger for the working sacrifice
raising strangers in loneliness

I hunger for New Orleans
I hunger for Biloxi
I hunger for Darfur
I hunger for Baan Nam Khem
I hunger for Fukushima
I hunger for Sandy Hook
I hunger for Parkland
I hunger for Haiti
I hunger for Puerto Rico
I hunger for Charlottesville

I hunger in the eye
of the oncoming future

Meditation in the Clouds

O sad night of the river
gurgling your emptiness to me

what sees you through the day?
a slap of truth
or half-eyed dream

is stability hard work
or can you fake it?

falling from mountains
to valleys
making the climb
for the sake of it

does nothing exist as it is

I want to lay on your shore
see the world
through a raindrop

rise to an illusion of being
still and silent
like trees in the blue dawn

was I born here
yesterday

when time walked
on crippled legs?

Without a Boat
for Li Po

on the bank
of the Star River

dipping in fingers
trying to catch the moon

Spelunking
for Tom Weigel

Here I am
            in Ted's city
Berrigan, of course

though you wouldn't know it
            from walking around
or visiting a library

this isn't Cleveland
            where they martyred d.a. levy
and for good reason
this is their home

Clark Coolidge
            walked these same sidewalks
with a jazz bop in his ear
like the words in his notebook
drumming down streets that now
            keep their poets hidden in caves
rather than displayed on bookshelves

Looking for Sunflowers

The tapestry of night

pinned by stars
           to the walls
turns in our sleep

the sidewalks tremble

narrow roads converge

street lamps
           shadow the homeless
& the late going home

the alabaster groaning
           in moon light
the neon slashes
           down faded alleys

lost saints
           wander the face of the city

not wanting to be found

sirens peek around corners

blue and red echo off brick

smoking philosophers
           scatting in doorways

rush of trains
           over the tide

the rain drops
           tip toe
           around conversations

before drowning in daylight

To Remain Alive

The fingers
of the leafless tree
scratch
at the flooded sky
as if intent
on tearing it
to pieces
and allowing
the ancient rain
to fall

Harsh Realities

Studying city streets
contemplating
worst case scenarios
chasing shadows
like dogs' tails

Dreaming of hotels
and the outside
hissing cars
waves on the night
floating in the current
going nowhere

You're lucky
to have died
on a train
at least
you're still moving

The Poet on Tilley St.

Shuffles along
the slumped streets
to his own mad jazz

red winter hat
floating like a halo
above his bobbing head

plaid sleeves
poke through cuffs
a coat of blue sky

he holds a plastic bag
that bounces with a back beat
in the shadow of Paris

Thinking of Delmore Schwartz

I disappear
from the light
and voices

hidden away
in a safety net

the world
laid out
with all
ignoble intentions

words are not read
in electric societies

the pillars
of ill-defined life
are all we hold
as truth

no end
no beginning
in between
we lie ourselves
into existence

Daybreak at the Intersection

I dance between dreams
on the edge of the moon

the emptiness
of sapphire streets

the lonely traffic light
flashing the only life

the sun in my eyes
four corners of uncertainty

Meditation at Daybreak

Here I am
walking these
uneven sidewalks
of my neighborhood
in the tossed shadows
of seaside morning

trying to clear my head
of all the rabble
that bounces around
like the few remaining
sailboats anchored
just off shore

and the sun
has grown tired
of holding long hours
and the air
cool off the water

cars coming and going
into the great void
of American living

the too blue sky above
empty of all clouds
and feelings
and all things
are beautiful
in that tired old sunlight
that begins to whither
like the wild flowers
that line the road

Neighborhood Sketch Just after Dawn

The sidewalk is quiet
in the early
angel morning

the sun reaching
peaking over
that giant ocean blue

the light swims to shore
arriving on the beach
like some silent wave
sending the tiny feet of night
retreating
like the final guests at a party

the sailboats are motionless
in the blinding sea
that reflects the stillness
of morning
like a clean mirror

birds chatter in the yard
over breakfast
like old men playing chess
in the park

Neighborhood Sketch in Morning

1.

    birds flutter
    in sunlit branches
    Friday morning coffee

2.

    birds in driveway
    dusty bath
    of feathers

3.

    over the water
    the sun marches

Old Highway Blues

On days like this
when the remaining
patches of snow melt

and the green grass
begins to pop through

and only seems green
because we haven't seen it
for a few weeks

and birds sing songs
in the still leafless trees

and a false spring
begins to climb out
of the sea
that was shimmering
with factory lights
just last night
under the stars
who twinkled
like little angel eyes
in the great void of space
and I know winter
still has a few months
of breath left in it

I think of those
great desert roads
that last as long
as they need to
and how they dive
over the horizon
only to begin again
like a new day

on the other side

and the old houses
with walls that have caved in
as if the last memory
that held them up
has faded away
slowly pass
in some sad vision
and I want to be driving
right now
in these frozen
New England months

knowing that each of these
holy strips of asphalt
paved with the dreams
of travelers
and old hobo ghosts
will continue to visit me
like an old friend
who has stopped by
for a drink

Oh City

Oh city of night
      death and happiness
        the beggars
        and homeless
        weep at your feet

Oh city of heartbreak
      loss and forgiveness
        the children play
        in your streets

Oh city of dreams
      pain and light
        the stars in the sky
        are drowned out
        by your noise

Oh city of love
      sing your song
        so we can dance
        together in the gutter

Oh city of night
      and light and pain and death
        blow your horn
        for tomorrow
        for today

        blow your horn
        for the lost ragged souls
        of the dark

Oh city of night
      blow your horn
        for us

On the Outskirts of Town

Down here
on the outskirts of town
in sleepy ol' America
sometime
after the sky has lost its blue

here I am
scribbling & giggling
in these tiny notebooks

the stars
peak over my shoulder
and the only thing
I can really hear
is a car
passing by
in the night
and maybe
a train whistle

writing by
the window light
or if I'm lucky
a full moon

I can see
the universe
spill out
before me

and here I am
floating through
the void
no more than
a leaf
down a lazy river
all peaceful & eternal

now the waves
hush
as they splash
on the beach below
and the constant
steady hum
of the factory
on the far shore

and I feel like
the last man
on earth
because the night
provides a certain
amount of loneliness

even when it's not
bleak and empty
but it's there
hiding out
in the shadows
ready to leap
if you turn your back

and I can feel it
as the pen
scratches words
onto the page
down here
on the outskirts
of town
in sleepy ol' America
where all the houses
are crowded with dreams

I Talked to the Moon

for Jack Micheline

I'm talking to the moon tonight
for you, Jack
   I moved my feet
   and made it to California
   a long way from home
I talked to the moon in Asheville
I talked to the moon in Nashville
I talked to the moon in New Orleans
where the waters rose
above the doors
but the bars did not close
   I talked to the moon in Texas
   in wide open spaces
   where poems rode
   like outlaws
   through the streets
   and the moon talked to me
   as it shined in the sky
   and reflected like
   the white line of the highway
   my insides spilled
   on the streets
   of Broadway in San Francisco
   my heart thumping
   in Chinatown
I talked to the moon
and rambled my dreams
and my nightmares
and the moon talked to me, Jack
the moon talked to me

Crazy Al,
Where Are You Buried?

I wonder to myself
on this bright afternoon
where do they bury the bums
that everyone knows by first name

Crazy Al
everyone greets him
with a smile and a
   "how ya' doin' pal?"

no one asked questions
when he disappeared
just the kids
who saw him on the streets
through car windows
on their way to Sunday school

they just kept on moving
assuming
he went someplace else
and finally decided
to leave town

is there an invisible cemetery
for all the invisible people
all over the world
to be buried in

do they have funerals
right in front of our eyes
down by the railroad tracks
asking each other
for cigarettes and wine
at the reception

bury me
in an invisible cemetery
with all the faces we don't see
and all the stories
we never heard

Jewett City Gangster

He walks down Main St.
in a black pinstripe suit
what Dillinger might have worn
the night he was gunned down

but now
it appears after years
of brawls and bad luck
closer to rags
than mafia-wear

he limps through town
suffering from the wound
left by the bullet
that found his leg
one night years ago
at the old hotel
down by the tracks

his drunken stubble
is what's left
of a three day binge

he pauses briefly
in a barroom doorway
swigs a pint
pulled from his pocket

squinting into the sun
scanning the sidewalk
always on the lookout
for the Lady in Red

Mohegan

Saturday morning
at the book
with my brother
a stable of grey faced
career gamblers all around
eyes screaming at TVs
horses gallop across screens
wrinkled hands gripping slips
that will fall to the ground
with each race
and flutter in the smoke
like broken dreams
in the wind
and us at the bar
just trying to get drunk
before lunch

Sing a Song

Early morning
sun in the sky
that big yellow bird
pulls up to the front walk
of the school
the doors open
a song falls down the stairs
with kids wearing smiles
out onto the front walk
and I ask the bus driver
why she sings songs with the kids
she brings to school
every day and home every night
and she said to me
> if they're singing songs
> they're not fighting

they're not fighting
and I sat down on a bench
with those words in my head
and I thought to myself
sitting in the sun
why can't rich old men
sing songs together
rich old men financing
all these wars
should sing songs together
and all the soldiers
all over the world
should sing songs together
as their bones are bleached
by the sun
out in the battlefields
and all the politicians

in all the countries
under the stars
can get together
and sing songs
they can all sing the same song
a song about the children
a song about the homeless
a song about the hungry
a song about the soldier
whose bones
are being bleached
by the sun
out in the battlefields

The Man in the Eye Patch

Arrives loud enough
for everyone to know
he has entered
as if still in his prime
yells
       "It's my birthday!"
but the crowd disagrees
he pleads his case between
handshakes and one liners
a politician
working the crowd
and finds his way
to our end of the bar
breaking into our huddle
he announces to my friends
with a tooth-filled grin
that it was his birthday
and that he noticed
we were not regulars
I buy him a whiskey
and his good eye told me
it wasn't really his birthday
as he drank his shot of sadness

Journeyman

The clouds attack
the sky
like a pack
of wild dogs
ripping and tearing
at the sun
as if it were
the last chunk
of meat
for miles around
tossing bits
and pieces
of sunshine
around the yard
that I'm laying in
on my back
knocked out
by a work week
that connected
to my chin
like a right hook
from the heavyweight
champ

Reflections from the Road

I cannot sleep tonight
stars scream in my eyes
the train horn tosses
and turns in my bed
invisible children
stomachs as empty
as their dreams
whimpering
in the rush of night
homeless clutching
cardboard resumes
and coffee cups
void of hope
fragile voices
asking my nightmares
for change

Poem for Hemingway
and Jack Hirschman

I travelled the country
by way of graveyards and back roads
the bones of outlaws and writers
and outlaw writers
piled up in mounds
their ghosts
walking the streets with us
hand in invisible hand
their words giving us
a private tour
of a forgotten country
the highways
stayed as long as the days
and the sun shined down
on Indian deserts
whose champions lay
in unmarked graves
the dark storm clouds
rained down
over the endless prairies
but their words were never
drowned out
the lakes and rivers
wrapped around us
high up into the mountains
where we twisted down
around curves
descending into a country
we never found

Poem to the Workingman

In all the cities
ancient buildings
of beauty rise upwards
along the streets
casting shadows
like colossal tombstones
legacies of the fortunate
erected with Cheshire grins
and fine cigars
counting their money
over imported whiskey
washing away their souls
until their bodies
were as hollow
as the creations
they financed
and now their bones
which held together
only skin
rot and decay
in the same earth
as the bones
of a thousand
ragged and broken men

Amor,
En Tres Partes

I.

If you
asked me
for flowers
I would
dig my fingers
into soil
and pluck them
from their
winter beds

II.

If you
asked me
for the sun
I would
swim out
to ocean's end
and heave it
burning upon
my back
and haul it
drowning in warmth
back to shore

III.

If you
asked me
for stars
I would
reach up and shake

the crescent moon
until they
came loose
and showered down
covering us
in cosmic dust

Proposition

Let's
go out
dancing
under
the street
lights
in the rain
and then
come home
and be
alone
for the night
let our
thoughts
swallow us
as we lay
tangled
in a
blanket
of stars

A Toast to Loneliness
for Dave Kennedy

To those who drink
lonesome in taverns
smoke streets brooding
with windblown eyes
slumped shivering in alleys
under the amber moon's
somber glow

to those wobbling
on heavenly rooftops
with cheap wine
and old friends
singing the sadness
of the stars

to those punching keys
in tenements
which are battered
worse than our souls
but still manage
to record the statements
that echo down boulevards
of the concrete dream

to those alcohol induced thoughts
floating up into the night
creeping out cracked windows
and down fire escapes
freezing with the dogs
on the rail

We scream at a new America

Advice

If you're planning on traveling
to the edge of the world
bring a change of clothes
you're going to get dirty
and bring a bottle
have a drink with whoever else
survives

On the Rocks

I drink
a glass
full of moonlight
to forget
the stars
beauty is painted
on the insides
of my eyelids
consuming
the cosmos
rotating
in a galaxy
where breathing
alone
is considered
a victory

Vagabond Blues

In the stillness
of night
wind chimes
fill the room
the train horn
blasts me back
to shadows
the passing
racket fades
into moonlight
my thoughts
ride the rails
across a distant
western prairie
where tonight
a freight train
a mile long
carries the dreams
of a thousand dead hobos
across the desert
to a rail yard in heaven

Nights at Mike's

We were
young dumb
and knew it all
higher than a hawks nest
in his parents basement
we'd change the world
and find ourselves
before it was all
said and done
we told anyone
that would listen
that someday
we'd cross
the country
together
they said
they'd been saying
the same thing
for 30 years
those words
were in my head
as the car
left his driveway
and we headed out
with the morning sun
in our rearview

Mountain Sketch

The river
smoothes
stones
and rushes
toward
twilight
clouds sit aloft
tops of mountains
like the old hats
of railroad men
the moon
has yet
to climb
over the ridge
an aged hiker
on a trail
to heaven

For Li Po

On this boat
watching
the sun set
on my youth
ten thousand
memories
shine like stars
in my heart
drunken moon
I love your smile
take me away
to lonely mountain
to cry in the arms
of trees
but here
on this river
the water kisses
constellations
and seems to whisper
farewell

Summer Night

I search
the yard
for any form
of life
but night
has collapsed
like the
final curtain
of a play
the stars
have gone their
separate ways
like strangers
at last call
disappearing
into darkness
no less alone
than before

Montauk by Morning

I walk
along Montauk
in the city
of New London
with love
in my heart
the early
morning sun
warms my back
trees line
the sidewalks
and drop shadows
at my feet
bicyclists and cars
dogs in the street
a train
blows its horn
like a thousand angels
the streets are alive
and so am I

Today in New London

for Tom Weigel

The jazz
of your poems
still echo
on city corners
and bounce
off battered
buildings

they race
down streets
on skateboards
and spill out
in conversations
at coffee shops
and taverns

they crawl
across yards
like the neighbor's cat
leaving footprints
in the snow

and they sing
like little birds
in the trees
whose leaves
have fluttered
in the wind
like your words

and I sit here
east of the sun
reading your books
and listening
to the rain

rattle the gutters
like your typewriter
rattling the night
as your poems
float out
onto the sidewalk
and sprout
like flowers
in the moonlight

At Ocean Beach

Two junkies
sitting
on a bench
shooting memories
in the sun
their smiles wide
as they get their
fix of the past
   "Man, it was like
   a blast of Buddhism
   she loved me
   when I played
   that song…"
and then
as if
reliving
a dream
a tourniquet
of words
wrapped around
his heart
and his voice
flatlined
as a child
left tracks
in the sand

Upon a Hangover

for Everette Maddox

One night
God
came to
visit me
he drank
all my whiskey
and told me
the universe
is an empty bottle

In the Funeral Parlor of the Mind

In the funeral parlor
of the mind

the dead sit smiling
passing a bottle

the morning sun
cuts asphalt

dreams bleeding
in the gutter

the undertaker
smiles

a mouth
full of razors

Nowhere Blues

Sometimes I dream
of a field

in a lonely
corner of life

sky pouring out
infinite, blue

barely a cloud

the sun, soft
barely a sound

a low buzzing
in the emptiness

nerve endings
in the breeze

Things I Can Do Before Bed

Before the night
rolls back
and the sun
rises up
with long fingers
and reaches over
the horizon
I can still
write these words
that will
make grey clouds
slip out to sea
like old iron sided
ghost ships
setting sail
for unknown ports

I can still
recite poems
to the trees
that stand naked
in moonlight
I can still
scratch words
on to paper
that will make
our leaders
collapse
at their knees
in fear

I can still
toss words
like seeds
out into

the arid winds
where they
carry softly
over walls
and grow
like flowers
along the borders

I can still
write words
that will draw
tears from stone
and before
morning light
crawls up
our bedroom walls
I can invite you
into my dreams
where the poems
write themselves
across night skies
and fade
like stardust
at dawn

Constantinople
Closed for Renovations

It's not a democracy
because they tell you
it's a democracy
though that's up for debate
the dumpster burning
in the alley
popped a rating
but was beaten
by an act of kindness
I said gimmee an old fashioned
not old fascism

Little Man

for Lawrence Ferlinghetti

There is
a little man
inside me
behind my eyelids
and crawling
across
my tongue
like a wounded
animal
there is
a little man
inside me
with fists
punching
the insides
of my ribs
screaming
in the chambers
of my heart
there is
a little man
inside me
with a
thousand faces
and as many voices
singing
the sorrow
from the sky
dancing the death
from view
a little man
who waves
no flags

and pledges
allegiance
to trees
and mountains
and the beauty
of life
America
I water
your parched throat
with the blood
of history
I kiss your cheeks
with the lips
of the poor
America
you've taken
all from most
and left
the rest
to raise
little men
and women
who will grow
and spread
resistance
like seeds
of wildflowers
in the wind

By The Fire

I don't know
what to believe
anymore

yeah
I'm on
your side

I just
don't know
what that
means
anymore

a floating
night of stars
or a film
projecting
emptiness

I feel

A certain
sense

of solitude
with night

so overrun
with stars

they are
under me

and around me
and now

I'm lost
holding onto

the moon
by one hand

dangling
in eternity

Last Petal

I saw
you there
on the outside
of a dream
holding on
to the fringes
of the seam
the night
itself
fell softly
on the yard
you walked
across
the day
and straight
into my eye
I blinked
but then
you multiplied
the sidewalks roll
like waves
before the beach
when the last petal
is about to
release it's hold
and float away
into the last
bit of sun
shining over
the neighborhood
and the garden
falls in
upon itself

standing below
a night
spilled over
with stars
my hands
are empty
with nothing
left to hold

Day to Day

We waste
our years
in the
rotation
around suns
no where
is far
enough
away
we dance
between
moon beams
thrown against
the bricks
of yesterday
all of us
alone
dancing
in rhythm
the star
dripped
nights
reflected
in puddles
a long
walk home
where ever
that is

Jake St. John writes out of New London Connecticut. He is a father, husband, teacher and Neo-Beat adventurer. His poems have appeared in magazines and journals around the world.

Thank you to the publishers and editors of the following:

Chapbooks
When I Was You (One Time Press, 2008)
Change of Address (Unarmed, 2010)
Looking for Sunflowers (Good Cop Bad Cop 2012)
Rotations (Night Ballet Press 2015)
In All the Cities The Same Faces (CWP Collective 2017)
Workingman's Odyssey (Analog Submission Press, 2018)

Magazines
Backroom Poets, Big Hammer, Fell Swoop, Unarmed, Burp, Flying Fish, Chronogram, Cokefishing in Alphabeat Soup, Elephant, Blue Collar Review, Big Hammer, Hobo Camp Review, Communicators League, The Rye Whiskey

Review, LipSmack, In Between Hangovers, Capsule, Concrete Meat, Rusty Truck, OZ-Burp, Street Value, Outlaw Poetry Network, Chopper, Your One Phone Call, The Cut Up, Wall-Of-Us, Oddball Magazine, Recession In Neverland, Up The River, , Spirit, Five Quarterly, Peoples Tribune, Spare Change, Oddball Magazine, unarmed journal, Poems-For-All, Sassafras Literary Magazine, Eternal Breakfast and The Scope

The Man in the Eye Patch was originally published in *The Chaffey Review, a literary journal VI*

Other Works from
A Jabber Publication

"Jon Dambacher (green)" by Jon Dambacher

"Jon Dambacher (brown)" by Jon Dambacher

"Buster" by Jon Dambacher

"Daffy" by Cliff Weber

"Scream as You Leave" by Ian Winterbauer

"Hearingaid!" by Jon Dambacher

Made in the USA
Middletown, DE
07 February 2019